DIARIES OF GENERAL FELIPE ANGELES
AND MAJOR FEDERICO CERVANTES

THE BATTLE OF ZACATECAS

JUNE 24, 1914

THE BATTLE OF ZACATECAS
JUNE 24, 1914

Diaries of
GENERAL FELIPE ÁNGELES and
MAJOR FEDERICO CERVANTES

Sharon Egger Heston
Translator

Wasteland Press

www.wastelandpress.net
Shelbyville, KY USA

The Battle of Zacatecas:
Diaries of General Felipe Ángeles and Major Federico Cervantes
Translated by Sharon Egger Heston

Second Printing – February 2024
ISBN: 978-1-68111-549-8

Printed in the U.S.A.

0   1   2   3   4   5   6

DEDICATION

This book is dedicated to my husband Leonard Heston. Without his encouragement and support this research could not have been accomplished.

ACKNOWLEDGMENTS

Locating these diaries and visiting the site of the Battle of Zacatecas was an outstanding adventure of this past year. Many people made it possible.

Thanks to the librarians at the University of New Mexico, Las Cruces and the El Paso Public Library. Both libraries have exceptional collections of Mexican revolutionary period material. One librarian, Gracie Garza, who has relatives in Zacatecas, told me that Zacatecas is a special place; this is no exaggeration. Claudia Rivers and her staff in the Special Collections of the University of Texas El Paso were also gracious and helpful.

In Zacatecas I was directed to the Historical Archives of the state of Zacatecas in the center of the city. Decades ago those archives were damaged by fire. Since that time a major effort has reconstructed and preserved valuable historical records. The facility is now state of the art: temperature and humidity-controlled in a fire protected structure.

The lovely, highly competent Director of the Historical Archives of the State of Zacatecas, Maria Auxilio Maldonado de Romero provided priceless resources and additionally she and her husband volunteered to guide us around the entire battlefield.

Thank you is an inadequate expression of the gratitude I feel toward them for their kindness and for sharing their expertise and their warm friendship.

I also want to express my gratitude to my grandson Sebastian Bolaños Heston who read parts of the book and provided valuable help.

CONTENTS

HISTORICAL CONTEXT

February 18, 1913.   A cabal within the federal army of Mexico arrests and jails elected President Madero.

February 22, 1913.   President Madero and vice President Pino Suarez are assassinated and General Huerta declares himself president.

March 1913.   The U.S. declares itself against Huerta.

April 1913   Venustiano Carranza, governor of Coahuila, is declared First Chief to fight against Huerta. Three divisions are established; one led by Alvaro Obregon, another by Pablo Gonzalez, and the third, the Northern Division, led by General Francisco Villa.

April 1914   General Felipe Ángeles joins General Villa to direct the artillery supporting the Northern Division.

June 23, 1914.   The Division del Norte (Northern Division) captures the city of Zacatecas.

July 15, 1914.   Huerta resigns as President and flees to the United States where he is arrested for conspiracy and held at Fort Bliss. He was released for health reasons and died of alcoholism in January of 1916.

PART ONE:
The Battle of Zacatecas
by General Felipe Ángeles

THE BATTLEFIELD DIARY OF GENERAL FELIPE ÁNGELES

Translated by Sharon Egger Heston

June 17, 1914:

Early Wednesday morning we began our journey from Torreón to Zacatecas, less than 200 miles but it would take two full days. My division went in five trains; four carried my troops and the fifth carried my staff, provisions and workers.

The first train left at 8:00 o'clock, the others at fifteen-minute intervals; however the fifth was delayed because of poor track conditions. It could not leave until two o'clock.

The journey was slow. Several rain showers made travel miserable for my troops who had no protection, not even raincoats.

June 19, 1914:

Friday morning, the 19th we arrived at Calera and disembarked immediately. Calera is about 25 kilometers from Zacatecas. The troops who had preceded me were waiting camped in the immediate area.

Because of the good faith and confidence that the general of the Division[1] had granted me, I took the initiative to reconnoiter and distribute soldiers around Zacatecas in positions near where they would participate in the attack.

General Chao, who had just arrived, came to visit me in my car and showed me where his troops would be camping. He also promised me an escort of 30 men to reconnoiter toward Morelos, "I myself, will accompany you," he said.

Three kilometers from Morelos we came across San Vicente, an abandoned *ranchito*. I sent some men to look it over. When we reached it I divided the escort into three parts to explore further: the main body

---

[1] General Francisco (Pancho) Villa, leader of the Division del Norte. SEH

was directed straight ahead toward the hills in front, another through a deep gully and on to some hills on the left, and the rest went toward Morelos.

Residents of this village and laborers in the fields that we were crossing, told us that they were fleeing from the enemy who had just come to Morelos, with the intention of burning forage and provisions; they pointed out silhouettes of mounted cavalry on the crests of the hills nearby and assured us that the shots we heard on the right were from the enemy.

Probably the enemy saw that we were few, perhaps they even counted us, for they decided to attack at a gallop firing shots against us.

We retreated slowly toward San Vicente observing the enemy all the while; when we reached a favorable place we dug in and engaged in a firefight for about half an hour. The enemy retreated in order.

As soon as those in the camp at Calera heard shots fired, General Urbina sent the intrepid General Trinidad Rodríguez with his Cuauhtémoc brigade to assist us. They swept the enemy from the hills in front of us.

We climbed there soon after.

From a high hill next to Morelos we saw a beautiful new landscape. In the distance the chapel of Vetagrande clung courageously to the mountainside and reached toward the skies; a little to the right were high and mysterious hills full of excavations…mines or fortifications; perhaps the enemy was hiding among them. More to the right and at our feet lay a carpet of green fields strewn with villages and trees. At the bottom of the hill dogs were barking and, wonderful sight, enemy soldiers were fleeing from our soldiers who pursued them headlong firing their rifles with great enthusiasm, a few were trying to cut off their retreat.

"It would be good", I said to General Trinidad Rodríguez, "if your troops could stay in Morelos and send scouts to those hills in front of us".

I am going to bring artillery and position it in Morelos.

Major Bazán went into town to scout positions for the artillery while the rest of us returned to Calera. I ordered artillery taken to Morelos. Carrillo's group left soon after

An officer came from General Monclovio Herrera to inform me that they had arrived and to ask me for instructions.

I went to see General Herrera; I told him I had not received orders to take charge of the troops in Calera, and that perhaps General Urbina had that command; but I would advise him to go to Cienaguilla, a place that had water and forage and was not yet occupied by other troops, a place favorable for his attack, when he was so ordered. I had no knowledge of Cienaguilla other than what I had learned from my guide and by letter. I promised to visit him the next day to study the terrain for the usefulness of the artillery and to decide how many pieces I should send him.

The groups of Saavedra, Jurado and Luévano also left for Morelos.

A formidable downpour fell and a strong wind began to blow. It was quite late when the three groups, my staff officers and I reached Morelos. I learned then that Trinidad Rodríguez had pursued the enemy beyond the batteries of Las Pilas and Hacienda Nueva, and that he had asked Carrillo's group for help attacking the enemy who had made a stronghold on the hill and the mines of Loreto.

June 20

I bathed in a miniscule tub.

General Pánfilo Natera came to greet me; he was mounted on a very small horse, but acceptable. We had breakfast together. He promised to accompany me with his escort and to guide me in today's reconnaissance mission.

Later we went to Vetagrande, a town once famous for its silver mines but now in sad condition, almost dead.

From the summit of the nearest hill we saw a beautiful panorama. To the right was the valley of Calera and Fresnillo, very large and much lower with many villages that seemed to dissolve in the radiant light of the morning. In front of us, a portion of the city of Zacatecas, between the two hills of El Grillo and La Bufa, which were two formidable, fortified positions. Between the two hills, in the far distance, behind the visible part of the city, was the hill of Clérigos. Behind La Bufa, under some vaporous clouds that looked like bursting bales of cotton, was a mountain plateau made blue by distance. To our left was a creek-bed that began almost at our feet and ended near Guadalupe, a village that is out of sight, but that I could visualize being behind a small cone-shaped hill. In the same direction and further away, a lagoon appeared as a mirror in the morning sun, on whose edges are pleasant groups of houses. And between us and Zacatecas, two rows of hills, one toward El Grillo and the other toward La Bufa. Separating the two were the ruins of an adobe village that in other times had been silver mine called La Plata

This spot is certain to play the most important part of the battle to come. I could not take my eyes from it. Little by little I headed for the future battleground; General Natera was close behind me, then Colonel Gonzalitos. A discreet 100 meters behind officers of the staff and their escort had dismounted, spread out, and were hidden on the other side of the high hill.

"It would be good," I said to the congenial General Natera, to bring our horses and move forward toward that deserted mine (the La Plata mine) and control it so we can see the battlefield better and more safely.

When the escort took the road to the city, the canons on La Bufa sounded repeatedly and then I heard firing from a fight in the mine that was finally taken by the escort commanded by Major Caloca. That young man dropped out of Military School at Chapultepec last year and came north in search of me.[2] Sr. Carranza, however, ordered him to stay with General Natera[3].

After a thorough inspection of the area, we walked a little further down the creek-bed that ended near Guadalupe then returned to Morelos to eat. I gave orders to Major Bazán to go toward Vetegrande and set up the first two artillery groups where they could cover El Grillo and La Bufa.

We dined well and pleasantly with General Natera and we agreed to meet at three o'clock in the afternoon to go and inspect the area around Cieneguilla, where the troops of generals Herrera and Chao were located.

About two o'clock I went to visit General Urbina in the (Morelos) Municipal building. Natera, Triana, Contreras, and other officers were with him. They had agreed that the troops of the last three generals mentioned as well as those of Banuelos, Domínguez and Caloca, would go to Guadalupe to take positions. General Natera told me that he was excusing himself from his commitment to accompany me on reconnaissance this afternoon. I informed Urbina that I am sending two groups to Vetagrande to place artillery by night in the spots I judge to be the most important part of the battle, and I asked him to send support troops to service the artillery. He sent me part of his brigade: the brigade commanded by General Ceniceros and a regiment from the Villa Brigade.

An envoy from General Herrera came to Morelos to look for me and remind me that I had promised to go to visit him to study the terrain and see how best to utilize the artillery. Major Cervantes, Captain Espinoza de los Monteros and I, went to San Antonio, where the troops of Herrera and Chao had advanced. The enemy artillery

---

[2] Following the assassination of President Madero in February of 1913 Felipe Ángeles broke with the federal army and joined the revolution to fight against the assassin, General Victoriano Huerta. Several of Ángeles admiring cadets dropped out of military school and went north to join him. SEH

[3] Ángeles is referring to a characteristic action by First Chief of the revolution, Venustiano Carranza, an arrogant man who needed to flaunt his power in petty ways. SEH

from El Grillo hit the ground we were crossing near the railroad and damaged a locomotive going from Pimienta to Fresnillo.

A locomotive derailed near Zacatecas. (Courtesy of the Historical Archives of Zacatecas.)

An official message from General Herrera, who we were using as a guide said, "It is safer here. By not taking precautions some officer and a soldier were wounded. Do you see where earth has been removed? That is a mine. There are a lot of *federales* (federal soldiers) there. They are very good shots".

My horse Ney is no longer lame and even without stretching his legs, his long stride and vigorous gallop are a delight.

We found General Herrera in San Antonio, inside a dark house full of officers stretched out on the floor. The general came out from among them with his usual good humor. "*Buenas tardes*, my general, we are leaving right now to explore the terrain and I am just waiting for my horse to be saddled. I will go on this one. Whose horse is this?"

We climbed a hill. "Careful, men, put your feet on the ground, (better walk) because they (the horses) make good targets from there."

We obeyed and walked to the crest of the hill; General Herrera remained on horseback.

In front of the small hill that we occupied was another valley, and then another larger hill that was infested by the enemy and dominated closely by El Grillo and La Bufa. On the right was the mountain of Clérigos, crowned by black dots (the enemy lurking in ambush) and more to the right was the mountain whose top was the high plateau that I had seen this morning behind La Bufa. There were black dots on that plateau as well. Were they friends or enemies? We did not know.

"Do you see that mine, my general?" they said to me. "That is El Rayo. And see those other houses, and the large corral? There are a lot of soldiers there; but send us a couple of canons and we will pound them until their tongues hang out. Wouldn't this be a good place to fire against those positions?"

"No, this is too far away," I answered. "I am going to send six canons that I have available, but don't place them here. At least place them on that hill in front of us, or better still over there, on the right side. The canons must be close so we can see clearly that they are hitting the enemy; and we must not fire when the infantry starts its assault. You know the artillery terrifies; when the canon roars, the enemy runs for cover and our infantry advances, and when the enemy dares to stick their heads out again our infantry is on top of them. The enemy abandons quickly. The enemy won't fire a shot at us."

We said farewell wishing to be together during the battle.

One officer accompanied us so that he could guide the way for the return of the artillery I would send.

Our return trip was quite different! It was a longer route especially for the horses. On the hill, La Sierpe, we heard persistent firing. From Zacatecas smoke rose to great heights. To me that suggested the federal garrison was going to abandon Zacatecas. I was informed that artillery could reach Guadalupe more quickly from General Herrera's position than from Vetagrande, and I thought that it would be better to send all of the third group to San Antonio, instead of the six pieces I had originally sent. If the *federales* retreated they would go by Guadalupe, and it would be necessary for General Herrera to have numerous artillery pieces in position in order to pursue them more effectively.

As we passed Las Pilas I gave orders to Major Carrillo to go immediately to San Antonio to be under the orders of General Herrera and support his attack.

We dined contentedly and slept happily.

June 21, 1914.

As I bathed I was a bit concerned because I did not know if the troops that were to support the two groups of artillery set up during the night between Vetagrande and Zacatecas, were well and effectively placed and going to be effective.

I ordered Col. Gonzalitos to take his battalion from Las Pilas to Vetagrande to help protect the artillery and I went in a bit of a hurry soon after together with my staff officers.

We had reached Vetagrande when a messenger from General Natera delivered a written message asking what I knew about that day's attack and what mission his troops were to perform.

I answered him, also in writing, that I did not believe that the attack would begin that day: mainly, because General Villa had not arrived and he would have to direct the battle; and secondly because some troops had not yet arrived and it would be a military mistake not to employ all troops available, and third, because not all of our munitions have arrived and we must not start a battle without reserve munitions.

"With regard to the mission of your troops," I told him, "I think when they attack Guadalupe the mission must be two-fold: first, to prevent the arrival of reinforcements from Aguascalientes by destroying the train tracks and detaching troops to stop reinforcements; second, to stop the exit of the garrison from Zacatecas by way of the road to Guadalupe toward Aguascalientes by positioning troops in Guadalupe and its surroundings. Both groups must be nearby to give each other support."

In the narrow streets of Vetagrande there was an accumulation of service cars for the provisioning of the artillery. I sent to look for places to lodge my staff and to establish a hospital. A few minutes later we went up the high hill to see the positions the artillery had taken.

The battery of Captain Quiroz had been designated to occupy the top of that hill; his service cars were obstructing the road; the movement of the battery was very slow due to the steep grade that required a double team of mules. We dismounted. Up ahead we saw two canons; their maintenance crews were straining as they labored over the wheels but finally they placed the canons in their definitive positions. Generals Trinidad and José Rodríguez came to greet me with the enthusiasm usual just before combat commences.

On the side of the hill away from the enemy there were many horses saddled and loose. They were to support the artillery that was being positioned. The enemy was cannonading our battery hotly; the maintenance crews were shielding themselves by lying face down on the ground behind small mounds of stone and the gunners worked cautiously because the enemy artillery had made a few hits. In a careless moment one gun carriage rolled backward, slowly at first, then faster. Some gunners tried to stop it but without success. The carriage began to roll over rapidly and was heading in the direction of the horses. It was impossible to stop it and everyone felt anguish for the horses who could be killed; but fortunately the carriage rolled to one side, bounced a few times, and reached the bottom of the abyss.

In the distance, wrapped in the brilliant clarity of the day, an immense valley could be seen dotted with small villages and covered with trees.

On the other side of the hill, in the direction of Guadalupe and atop the ruins of La Platera mine, I could see five batteries, with their gunners immobile behind plates of armor, Some were making trenches to provide better cover from the persistent fire of the adversary. The batteries had received orders to take position but not fire even though being fired upon.

Further to the right in the mine of the hill of Loreto, the enemy battled the brigades of Villa and Cuauhtémoc on their flank, who were spread out along the crest below us. Even further away, ascending the crest of La Sierpe, looking like the spine of a huge animal inhabited by a row of black dots; they were visible from where we were but hidden, except for their heads, from the side of Hacienda Nuevo and Las Piles where we had our troops.

The canons of El Grillo and of La Bufa thundered constantly and our stationary artillery were receiving enemy grenades. Directly across from our position, Chao and Herrera were being battered.

In the afternoon we set up a hospital in the lower part of our camp, visited the advanced batteries, and chose places to help the wounded.

It rained cruelly on our gunners who had no raincoats.

As we returned to Vetagrande, we heard the piercing cries of the gravely wounded and saw the dead stretched out in the patio lying on stretcher, faces covered with handkerchiefs.

Someone reported to me the great destruction done by two shells, one from the enemy that had hit in the heart of the battery of Quiroz and another of our own that had exploded in the hands of a gunner as he put in the firing pin.

The Schneider-Canet canons would not return to their carriages after a few functional shots. Major Cervantes left on foot for San Antonio in the middle of the night in search of Lieutenant Perdomo to repair the brakes. After an exhausting hike, Cervantes returned to Vetagrande at three in the morning with Perdomo.

June 22, 1914

I woke early concerned by the rains that had fallen on my soldiers, and about food service for the artillery that was not as satisfactory as I wished and wondering why the brakes on the Schneider-Canet canons were not functioning well; perhaps because the workers had loaded them badly or because projection charges of the projectiles were defective.

General Felipe Ángeles. (Courtesy of Special Collections of University of Texas El Paso.)

I advised Barzán to order an improvement in the food service. I spoke to Perdomo and Espinosa de los Monteros about fixing the brakes of the Schneider-Canet canons, and I ordered Major Ángeles to establish a first-aid station for the wounded.

I learned that the Zaragoza brigade had arrived in Morelos under the command of General Raúl Madero, and I left for that town with the object of bringing his brigade to Vetagrande. But speaking with General Urbina in Morelos, I learned that the Zaragoza brigade was on its way to another position and it would be Raúl's responsibility to visit the positions near Vetagrande.

Going along the road to the mine we ran into an officer who told us that General Urbina had modified the order for the Zaragoza brigade, in the sense that it would be outside the terrain occupied by the artillery, proving to me once again General Urbina's tactful efforts to keep everyone happy without prejudicing the service.

With Raúl I visited the battery of Quiroz from where I showed him the positions of all the canons. After lunch Raúl went to inspect his troop.

I was walking over to inspect the artillery when Lieutenant Trucios let me know me that General Villa had just arrived and was coming to see us.

We saw him, friendly and enthusiastic as always, mounted on the spirited little horse of General Urbina.

I offered to show him battlefield positions. We went to see the batteries and when we advanced further Gonzalitos met us and guided us by way of the best protected roads. In the ruins of La Plata mine we examined the large yards in preparation of advancing the batteries through them during the night. I ordered Espinosa de los Monteros to bring Major Jurado so I could show him the positions that his three batteries must take that night. I showed Saavedra the position for one of his near the village next to the mine in front of La Bufa. Gonzalitos pointed out to me another very good position from which we could fire on La Bufa as well as the hill next to it; and I commissioned him to notify Saavedra and order him to take that position during the night.

On the way back I took General Villa to the position of Quiroz. From there I showed him the entire battlefield. He told me, "You and Urbina will enter through there, in front of the batteries. I will come from the right flank, and also attack the hill of Loreto." Urbina recommended that the battery of Quiroz fire on a hill that flanked the troops of General Villa's, which would be attacking Loreto.

As I was leaving, General Villa ordered me together with the Zaragoza brigade to relieve the part of Morelos that would support the artillery.

We ordered the Zaragoza brigade to advance in broken formation. There was one exposed area and there we ordered the troops to pass in small groups and at a gallop. In the creek bed behind our position that had the artillery the troop of the brigade dismounted and formed on foot.

Madero, Major Ángeles, Cervantes, Espinosa de los Monteros and I advanced to show the officer in charge the positions that his troop must relieve.

The night was damp, cloudy and very dark. The only light was from the spotlight atop La Bufa that turned continuously, stopping occasionally to illuminate terrain it vainly wanted to explore.

In spite of the fact that I had been over the area various times in the daylight, tonight I had difficulty. Several times I stepped into pools that had formed from the heavy rainfall. Fortunately we met a boy from our vanguard that guided us.

Our return was difficult. Sometimes the limited light from the spotlight seemed to follow us. At last we found troops from the Zaragoza Brigade on foot and they pointed out where our horses were. We mounted and left for Vetagrande under a light rain by the shortest road, not the one used before because at that time we had needed go out of formation.

Only our guide was able to follow the road, the rest of us walked carefully in his footsteps, trusting and silent. It was a procession of ghosts, stretching alongside an enemy who dreamed nightmares lying there beneath that spotlight that was nothing but a symptom of fear; serving no purpose other than to make one believe that it was accomplishing something.

We dined gaily in the company of *don* Angel Caso and two doctors from the medical service of the Zaragoza Brigade. The former asked me where the battle would be fought the following day.

We slept well.

June 23, 1914

We woke late, I shaved, bathed and changed my under clothing; we breakfasted and mounted our horses; I was riding my Curely, brilliant and muscular.

An aide of Colonel Gonzalitos came asking written instructions; I gave them and repeated them verbally when Gonzalitos and I met later.

We went to see General Ceniceros to explain his mission in the combat. He and Gonzalitos were to take the hill of black land next to La Bufa, under cover of fire from the batteries of Saavedra. Raúl Madero would take the hill of red soil (that of Loreto), under the cover of the batteries of Jurado at the same time that the troops with General Villa would be attacking from the right.

We left our horses protected from bullets and advanced on foot to the ruins of La Plata mine.

Overnight our artillery had disappeared from their original locations and taken other positions much closer to the enemy but hidden from their sight. Three batteries (of Jurado's group) were located inside the large corrals of La Plata mine. One of Saavedra's was next to the ruins on the plain, but behind the crest of a minute hill in front of La Bufa; another on the extreme left, also in front of La Bufa but well protected behind a crest; a third battery of the Saavedra group remained on the high hill of Vetagrande

The enemy must have been surprised at the disappearance of our batteries that had been silent for two days in spite of rifle bullets whistling by them like speedy mosquitoes.

Inside the large corrals we found Raúl Madero; "All is ready my General", he said, "but it is not quite 9:00 o clock. At 10:00 o' clock we must begin the battle."

Engineer Enrique Valle came running and told me, "I come to put myself at your orders for what ever I can do to serve. Do you understand me?"

An officer from General Aguirre Benavides told me that the Robles Brigade was awaiting orders from someone. "It would be helpful," I answered, "to use you as reserve." But later I decided his troops would be more useful attacking the hill of the black earth, and I invited him to join General Ceniceros and Colonel Gonzalitos.

I ordered all the *jefes* (officers) to present themselves and I reiterated orders for the attacks. In only twenty more minutes everything had to be in place, ready to fire at precisely 10:00 o'clock.

In the distance, from the direction of Hacienda Nueva, we heard the first gun shot. There came General Villa! The battle had begun!

The twenty-four canons closest to us, positioned between Vetagrande and Zacatecas roared, their projectiles ripped the air with shrieks of death and exploded, some on the hill of black soil, others on Loreto. The very depths of the mountains next to us seemed to explode a thousand times with the echoes. And the infantry troops advanced over the emerald mantle that covered the slope.

On the side of San Antonio, there by the high plateau and by the Villa de Guadalupe, canons and rifles and thousands of whistling projectiles thundered. Echoes from the mountains prolonged the sound of detonations, like yards of cloth being ripped on their flanks.

That epic concert intensified as additional canons thundered from Zacatecas, El Grillo, La Bufa, the hill of Clérigos, and all the federal positions.

Enemy shells began to explode in our direction; but they were high and very long.

Someone said that they believed we were too far away, behind the protective walls; another assured us that the federals were firing on our cavalry that had entered the action from the right. Other shells fell behind us, perhaps shot over the closest battery of Saavedra.

Another came running to inform us that a battery to the right of Jurado was being hit by enemy artillery; another said that two mules had been killed as well as one grenade thrower; a third had taken down the main piece of the nearest battery, that of Saavedra.

"Come and see, my General, through here, through this space, see how almost all the blows fall behind the battery. The first piece is now unmanned and the others are immobile behind the armor." The shells of the enemy were zooming and exploding in the air launching their sheaf of shrapnel or rebounding with a dry blow that exploded later sending their shrapnel forward into the earth or the rocks on the ground; a tragic and terrorizing hurricane.

I returned to my original observation point where I could not see the effect of the batteries that fired against the hill of black soil but where I could perceive the effect of the battery that battered the red hill, the hill of Loreto.

Perhaps there where the red soil had been removed our shells would also blow their tragic hurricane; but from our viewpoint we just seemed to be tickling the enemy. After a few minutes it seemed our shells were falling on abandoned parapets and trenches because the little black dots that moved around at first on the red soil had now disappeared.

Our soldiers were shouting with joy!

"Look at our men! How close they are to the enemy. See, the most forward flag is ours!

"Look! Look! Look what is happening! See how they are running away!"

The canons lengthened their shots and our infantry began a furious attack. The tri-color flag was raised in the position of conquest. It was only twenty-five minutes after ten in the morning.

A short time later, the flank of access to the hill of Loreto was populated with our infantry that climbed slowly and painfully; the horses were also arriving slowly. Later all could be seen in formation and protected.

The time had come to change our position. I asked Major Cervantes to order our horses brought so we could go survey Loreto to decide the best route to take and the next placement of Jurado's group of canons.

Captain Durón was shelling effectively in the intermediate position between Loreto and El Grillo. I authorized him to continue.

As I galloped with my staff toward Loreto, we met General Villa and his retinue; He came on his powerful red saying that he needed artillery sited in Loreto. "It's on the way my general," I replied. We proceeded along the road to Loreto.

General Francisco Villa on horseback. (Courtesy of the John O. Hardman Collection.)

Did the enemy realize that General Villa would be travelling in a group such as ours? Perhaps; at least they guessed that this joint meeting of two groups of staff officers was important because the path of their firing followed us. The *Jefe* took charge and we obeyed. Who fell on the road? We hoped it was not General Villa. Bullets whistled by, encrusting the ground.

The horse of Major Barzán was injured on one hoof and his assistant was injured on his arm.

In Loreto the rain of shells was heavy. Where did they come from? Who knew? But I did not try to fire on my mysterious enemy. All our attention was focused on helping the infantry attack of General Servín who was climbing up the sides of the hill La Sierpe and was at the point of being thrown back.

All our troops from Loreto were firing against the summit of La Sierpe without helping Servín it seemed. General Villa established a machine gun in an angle of a house and also opened fire on the summit of La Sierpe, but that did not facilitate the advance of Servín either.

And the artillery did not arrive; the minutes seemed like hours!

At last a canon came and then others from the command of Durón. The first canon blast sounded happily in our ears and probably very disagreeably in the ears of the defenders of La Sierpe. That first shot was on target and boosted the morale of our troops coming from Loreto, and after fifteen minutes the enemy began to evacuate their position; Our tri-color fluttered on the summit and our soldiers began shouting frenetic, enthusiastic hurrahs. The entire infantry of Servín scrambled up the pine-covered sides of La Sierpe to that much-desired summit.

And because this summit dominates El Grillo, taking it was the second step in conquering the strongest position of the enemy.

The canons that battered Sierpe could not be used from the same position to attack El Grillo: I had to place them to the front of the houses, in a small patio that had a circular wall facing the enemy with openings the canons could use. But that side of the houses was blasted by a hurricane of death. Bullets from rifles whistled rapidly and the shells exploded thunderously. Very few bodies remained erect; few heads remained high.

I gave the order to Captain Durón to bring artillery and place them in battery mode in front of the houses, where the machinegun used to be, and a little later I sent the remaining pieces to the left.

It was on that side, behind the houses that I found a disorderly mound of soldiers, horses, carriages, artillery with shells that were unfired, but without operators or officers.

It was difficult to make operators and officers reappear and move the canons to the patio I mentioned. They had to cross a narrow road that was very visible to the enemy and a perfect distance for their artillery. It was necessary to use my revolver and muster the fiercest energy.

The same persuasion that moved the artillery also moved the straggling infantry. Men advanced with backs bent in an effort to be protected by the circular wall. From there we pushed them toward the enemy showing them as an example the rest of the infantry that was battling the enemy a thousand meters further ahead. The forced charge by our straggling infantry was very interesting. It seemed that a formidable wind blew in their face and made them fall back when they were ordered to advance. Bless the soldiers of the village, obliged by duty to be heroes they advanced although their souls trembled and their knees weakened!

One battery remained in that patio, a battery that kept firing at El Grillo in spite of receiving fire not only from that artillery but also from above, from La Bufa.

If they drove us back from Loreto, if they drove back the artillery, it would not be possible for our infantry to continue on El Grillo: it was necessary to rush boldly, in spite of the violent fire of the enemy that was almost entirely concentrated on Loreto. The artillery, a moment earlier terrorized, was newly fired up and courageous. Now they were working heroically in the middle of a rain of lead and steel.

General Villa stood on a pile of stones to follow the work of the artillerymen attentively as well as the slow and painful progress of the infantry and the feverish activity of the enemy. They could feel their defeat coming in the violent advance of the Division del Norte, though maybe not the great catastrophe of the great final graveyard that loomed. Suddenly there was a huge explosion. Three meters from us there was a cloud of smoke and dust. There were shouts of terror. We thought an enemy bomb had hit point blank on the spot next to us and had killed all the operators.

When the smoke and dust had dissipated we saw various dead, one with two hands blown off, blood congealing on bones of his forearms, his head gone and belly destroyed and clothing blackened, he lay immobile, as if he had been dead for hours. Another indelible impression was that of a wounded man who had the face of a ghost and a thread of blood pouring from half open lips that were trembling in pain.

It had not been an enemy bomb; but a one of our own shells that exploded as the crew prepared to fire it. We could not allow our artillerymen to reflect on the danger of handling grenades. It was necessary to distract them by whatever means.

"Nothing happened," I shouted at them, "Don't stop! Some must die, and some must live. To live we must kill the enemy. Fire without ceasing!"

The fire continued stronger than before. General Villa stepped back a few steps and lay down on a heap of sand. He said to me sadly, "You don't know what pain the death of one of my boys causes me. When the enemy kills them, it happens; but death from our own weapons causes me pain".

"What shall we do," he continued, "so that our infantry can continue to advance? They seem to me a bit broken."

"They are very tired", I answered, "and one single advance is not going to dislodge the enemy from all their positions. Would you like Cervantes to order the infantry to advance?" Cervantes left us, happy to be used on this mission.

We could see him afar, with his hat tilted to one side, galloping rhythmically on his sorrel horse.

General Raúl Madero said that his troops were exhausted and he requested fresh troops to launch the attack on El Grillo.

My assistant, Baca brought food that we shared with General Villa and the other officers there. We ate contentedly sitting inside a large house with a roof that looked like a sieve because of holes made by our shells. I had never seen that much destruction with so much pleasure.

To aide our digestion Cervantes and I went for a walk. We came across a severely wounded horse that moved us with pity. We put him out of his pain. The detonations of our pistols seemed faint to our deafened ears.

The noise of the battle became more perceptible as we drew closer and we returned with rekindled passion.

I knew almost from the beginning of the attack that my battery had to leave the position that was attacking La Bufa and move in order to attack El Grillo.

Where was Gonzalitos? What was he doing? Had he eaten? Was he wounded?

I decided we would move to the other side of the battlefield and left a message for General Villa explaining my departure.

I sent an order to Captain Quiroz to leave the high hill at Vetegrande and move to El Grillo where he would receive further orders. I felt certain that in the time it took Quiroz to move, El Grillo would be in our power.

We were enjoying a gallop on our horses, when Gonzalitos appeared limping. He had dislocated his foot. "Yes sir, I have eaten," he told me with a smile.

All was going well on that side; the slope of the black soil hill was taken earlier and now those soldiers were fighting with those defending La Bufa.

I gave the command for one of the batteries of Saavedra to advance to the slope that was on the backside of the black soil. From that place we had an admirable view of Zacatecas, La Bufa and the road from Zacatecas to Guadalupe. On the other side of Zacatecas, between La Bufa and El Grillo, were troops, probably those of Herrera, Chao and Ortega. They had taken over a white house with a large corral adjacent to it.

Near our position there were some straggling infantrymen, those who always found some excuse to stay behind.

The battery of Saavedra settled into the new position and opened fire on La Bufa.

Now the fight took on the aspect of the complete victory to come. The resistance from La Bufa and El Grillo was weakening. I could see it was just a question of time until the idea of defeat germinated in the mind of the enemy.

Yellow smoke soon arose from the city as if it were mixed with dust. Perhaps it was a fire, perhaps an explosion. We checked our watches: it was 5:50 in the afternoon.

Our troops were encircling the enemy and tightening the noose. What was the enemy going to do? Where did they intend to retreat?

Engineer Valle, Major Cervantes, my brother[4] and I saw many troops on the road from Zacatecas to Guadalupe. It pleased us to be able see them so distinctly.

Meanwhile the enemy could be seen; soldiers in groups and others trying to get into formation. Then we noticed a thin line of infantry that preceded the cavalry, formed into a dense column. What did they intend? Perhaps they were going to retreat? But in that formation! We saw them advance toward Guadalupe, and then retreat in disorder. They could not discern our troops who were driving them back.

Soon the enemy moved toward Jerez, and then retreated. They were intending to go through Vetagrande, on the side where we had sent the stragglers to hunt them.

"Don't worry", I told them, "they are not going to fight, they are going to hide. They have nothing to do but exterminate them. The enemy will be turned back."

Finally they seemed to be making one final desperate retreat in the direction they had originally chosen, the road toward Guadalupe. And they were in almost complete disarray. We did not see their fall, but we could imagine it. I confess without shame, that if I saw them annihilated it would have given me the greatest delight; because I saw it from the point of view of an artist, the success of a completed work, a finished masterpiece. And I sent to General Villa this message: "We

---

[4] Major Ángeles was the general's younger brother. SEH

have won, my General"! And effectively the battle was over even though there were many shots still to be fired.

In the distance to the South, the battlefront of generals Herrera, Chao, and Ortega, the place where the white house and large corral were located, the flash of priming shots from the resplendent canons looked like tiny shards of mirrored glass.

Little by little the black dots began to descend from El Grillo running toward the City

Below us at the edge of the road to Vetagrande we saw a dam with clean blue water next to some peaceful houses. We walked down to see it, no longer concerned about the outcome of the battle.

As we were rejoicing about the batteries on our left, we could hear the canon blasts better from those to our right, they were firing against El Grillo; from whose crest the federal troops were retreating slowly and apparently tranquilly.

A great quiet reigned in the abandoned houses next to the dam, disturbed only by the braying of a couple of donkeys. Once in a while, a bullet would zoom by, lost no doubt.

Major Cervantes, at the side of Engineer Valle and of Major Ángeles, stretched out on their bellies on the ground, supported behind by their toes and in front by their elbows with their sombreros half off their heads so that, between the houses of picturesque Zacatecas, they could see the details of combat in the camp opposite on La Bufa. Or further away near the white house next to the corral, they could see some silhouettes of horsemen and the colorful group of Carrillo's batteries.

Margarito Orozco, the courageous and maimed enthusiast, galloped up on his spirited horse." *Buenas tardes* my general, it seems we are going to leave soon"

I dismounted and we walked around the pond and sat on the wall of the dam to talk of our ideals of happiness for the whole world. I was enchanted by the great and good soul of my friend.

One of our soldiers came from Zacatecas dying of thirst. He drank by lifting water to his mouth in his hand. The afternoon breeze brought the stench of a dead horse a few steps away

I returned to join my group of assistants and saw the top of El Grillo filled with our troops who came down from right to left above Zacatecas and I also saw that our troops had begun to enter La Bufa from the left.

Now, I thought, we lack only the final phase, the disagreeable part, our entrance into the conquered city bringing death to the straggling enemies who are going to leave this world filled with terror.

Cervantes and Valle wanted to see this phase of the battle: I commissioned them to go into Zacatecas right away to look for lodging for troops and officers. Meanwhile, I went to Vetegrande to arrange for moving the hospital and kitchens.

Captain Espinosa de la Monteros was commissioned to carry the order for the batteries to move to Zacatecas and stay wherever Major Cervantes indicated, an order that was received with happy hurrahs.

It was 6:45 in the afternoon. The temperature was delicious and the sun of the glorious day of June 23rd died peacefully.

I returned with my brother and my aide. We could now walk tranquilly through terrain that had been in enemy hands for so long and a few hours ago had been furiously contested. The main street of Zacatecas was visible through an entry raked by enemy shells.

"Boys, you can now go to Zacatecas: the city is ours," I told soldiers that we were meeting on the road.

Doctor Wichman vacillated at first and followed us at a great distance, but at last decided to enter Zacatecas later that evening.

In Vetagrande they received the news of the triumph with great gusto.

Stretched out peacefully on my field cot I revisited the phases of the classic battle; a miracle given the untrained revolutionary troops who had been organized and instructed even as they were assembling.

I reviewed the principle attack made on the lines of La Bufa, El Grillo and the front by the troops of Ceniceros, Aguirre Benavides,

Gonzalitos and Raúl Madero, supported by the artillery and the flanking troops of Trinidad and Jose Rodriguez, of *don* Rosalio Hernandez, Almanza and the entire infantry: all together ten thousand men.

When the principle defense was demolished, and the garrison could no longer continue to resist because La Bufa and El Grillo dominated the city, they tried to escape via the Southern route or by the East. However, exit to the South was impractical because the lines of communication were to the East by way of Guadalupe toward Aguascalientes. Three thousand of our men were enough to prevent the retreat by that route. In contrast, in Guadalupe a strong reserve was necessary, seven thousand men centered in Guadalupe plus troops on the flanks, obstructed the retreat through Jerez and Vetagrande. It was there we gave the final blow to the enemy already demoralized by the main attack and ready to abandon the city.

And in the development of the action: what adjustments and what harmony in the collaboration between the infantry and the artillery! The artillery worked in unison with the exclusive object of hitting and neutralizing the enemy in the positions our infantry wanted to conquer. Only one battery was used against an opposing battery and the infantry moved resolutely on the position after neutralization had been accomplished. What satisfaction to have reached this cooperation of arms so recently initiated in San Pedro de Las Colonias with Madero and Aguirre Benavides. So much perfection after the confusion of Torreón, won by force, tenacity and courage! And I had to appreciate how the whole world needed this kind of harmony and cooperation.

I reviewed the battle condensed into one attack using two branches of our army in a harmonious concert: the retreat to the South blocked, and the reserve to the East able to give the *coup de gras* to the enemy in disarray.

And over that theoretic concept that summed up a great battle plan, I collected episodes that impressed me the most: the precision of the battle's phases: the impetuosity of the attack; the hurricane of steel and lead; the explosions of armaments multiplied to infinity by echoes that simulated a cataclysm; the heroic force of the weak souls that moved hunched over against the tempest of death; the sudden and tragic deaths following the explosion of the shells; the wounded full of fear and immense horror that saw the implacable approach of death; the heroics of the wounded like Rodolfo Fierro spouting blood, forgetful of his own person yet able to participate effectively in combat; or the wounded that were unable to continue the fight who sadly left the battle like the intrepid Trinidad Rodríguez, who was surprised by death while life was telling him lovingly, "Don't go, it is not time yet". So many things, many beautiful things; and finally, in the afternoon, serenity with the full certainty of victory that came with a loving smile to caress the face of Francisco Villa the brave and glorious soldier of the people.

Under the enchantment of the classic masterpiece of that happy day, I sank placidly into a restorative dream without apprehensions.

June 24, 1914

On the following morning we entered Zacatecas visiting the battlefield on the side near La Bufa; squadrons of vultures had been hard at work on the enemy.

There were few dead there; but almost all were atrociously wounded and their positions revealed a painful agony.

Looking like looters we scavenged for useful equipment and munitions. We stationed vigilantes to guard the things we wanted and sent troops to retrieve them.

Inside the city there were many more dead, invariably with wounds to the head.

The accumulation of our soldiers made all parts of the streets impassable.

Ruins of a building, the Department of Armaments, filled the cross streets. They said that in the city entire families had perished in the destruction of that building, blown up by federal troops for what reason I don't know.

Ruins in the city of Zacatecas, June 1914
(Courtesy of the Historical Archives of Zacatecas.)

There were so many troops in Zacatecas that Cervantes could not find anyplace to billet the artillery and he decided to look in the direction of Aguascalientes, in Guadalupe, or further toward the lagoon of Pedernalillo whose mirrored surface we had seen the first time we climbed the high hill of Vetagrande.

Oh! The road from Zacatecas to Guadalupe: an infinite tenderness oppressed by heart. What caused me such joy the evening before because it indicated an unequivocal triumph now moved me deeply.

Both sides of the road were filled with cadavers, to the extent that it was impossible for carriages to pass on the seven kilometers of road between Zacatecas and Guadalupe and the regions nearby, both sides of the road were filled with cadavers to the extent that it was impossible for carriages to pass. The bodies lying there amounted to at least eighty percent of those federals killed.

Dead horses had neither saddles nor bridles and the soldiers had neither weapons, nor shoes. Many did not even have clothing.

The quality of the underclothing revealed that many of the dead had been officers.

Thanks to the cold temperatures of Zacatecas, the cadavers did not even smell and it was possible to observe them without repugnance.

All the horses were inflated with gases their legs rigid and separated. Looters had already been at the soldiers removing shoes, and exterior clothing. Facial expressions of the dead varied widely. Those who died peacefully only seemed to be sleeping, but some remained in attitudes of desperation with grimaces of pain and terror. I thought that the major part of the dead were probably enemies of Huerta and could have been friends of ours. And I knew that some of them were my friends. Only the inertia of the herd had kept them on the side of injustice!

In Guadalupe (as in Zacatecas) the residents were terrified. Would their properties be respected? One said, "It is all right to allow the soldiers what ever they want, but respect my life and that of my wife and children".

One woman had a premature birth and had died of fright.

All asked safe conduct and all disputed the honor of inviting the main officers to dinner so that they would give them guarantees.

The war for us, the officers, was full of charms that produced infinite sadness and shame; but everyone must see it as part of his job. What for some is calamity, for others is a great art.

I stayed in the mine La Fe with my general staff; the troop stayed in Guadalupe.

We were very grateful for the comfortable hospitality that the Noble family gave us.

June 25, 1914

Mounted on my Turena who leaped gracefully over walls and wide ditches, I went to see General Villa and requested four brigades of cavalry to take Aguascalientes. "I am going to give you seven, my general." And he gave orders to the *jefes* of those seven; and I gave mine the order to leave the following day. Eagerly I rubbed my hands together; I was certain that on Sunday we would enter Aguascalientes.

General Felipe Ángeles. (Courtesy of the John O. Hardman collection).

But fate had other plans.

Our commander had been sleepless thinking of the situation of the Division del Norte.

Confidant that the rest of the Constitutionalist fighters had little enthusiasm to go South toward México City, we were moving ahead quickly, but because of two great battles (Torreon and Zacatecas) we had no munitions; we were not allowed to bring munitions through Ciudad Juarez; neither would our friends allow us to go to Tampico for arms, nor would Carranza allow us to get coal from Monclova.

Licenciado Miguel Alessio Robles was sent from the army of the North East to initiate talks with us. He informed us that their attitude was entirely harmonious and if we disobeyed the order that General Villa give up the command of the Division of the North, it would bring due consequences very harmful to the cause and to the nation that we were obliged to avoid. He demanded that we make no further plans for a rapid march to México City and that we invite the Army of the Northeast to go San Luis Potosí.

The response to Licenciado Alessio Robles was to decline the invitation. And our return to the North became indispensible.

After the Pact of Torreón when we came to appreciate the transcendent importance of the Battle of Zacatecas we thought we could easily enter the capital of the Republic. If it became necessary for us to help the revolution we would go South, but for now it was more important to go North to avoid provoking a new crisis.

July 8, 1914

It was sad and at the same time comfortable to ride on our trains over the fields of the State of Chihuahua!

A rapid parade of posts and bushes is passing by the square of the window across from which I write these notes on my knees.

*****

TOPOGRAPHICAL MAP OF
ZACATECAS DRAWN BY MAJOR
FEDERICO CERVANTES

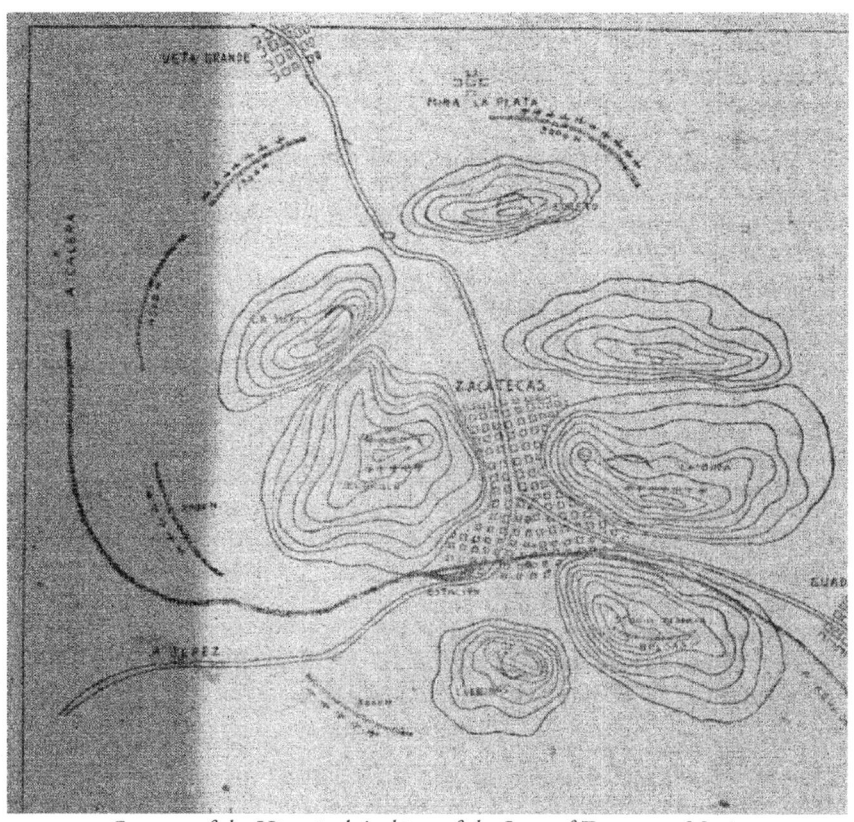

Courtesy of the Historical Archives of the State of Zacatecas, Mexico

PART TWO:

The Assault and Capture of Zacatecas

by Major Federico Cervantes

THE BATTLEFIELD DIARY OF MAJOR FEDERICO CERVANTES

Translated by Sharon Egger Heston

Action alone reveals the nature of our intelligence and the valor of our character.

Gustavo LeBon

More than once we have seen that when men of action attained prestige for their deeds Venustiano Carranza felt his overarching ambition threatened and his glory overshadowed. But never before was that purely ornamental figure of the Revolution made more envious than when Pancho Villa, faithful friend of Madero, escaped from prison and the death planned for him by Victoriano Huerta.

When Villa escaped he fled across the northern border to El Paso and returned to Mexico with only a fistful of pesos and eight men to form an army and grow in military prestige to the extent that he caught worldwide attention; that lifelong fighter was a celebrated guerilla, from guerilla he became a tactician, and from tactician a strategist.

Chihuahua:

General Felipe Ángeles summarized Villa's campaign with eloquent lines: "With insufficient troops and munitions he attacked Chihuahua from the east. Pretending that his attack had failed he marched by night, encircling Chihuahua to be able to attack to the north by rail. He commandeered a train and with sharp attention to detail he misled the enemy in Ciudad Juarez, who until the train actually arrived in the heart of that city, believed him to be near Chihuahua. He surprised the garrison and destroyed it. Meanwhile he marched the rest of his troops on foot to Ciudad Juarez to slow down his enemies and give himself time to equip and rearm. Because of the proximity of Ciudad Juarez to the United States, Villa came at the federalists in a manner that would avoid international complications[5]. Following that victory he destroyed Nuevo Blanco and continued toward Chihuahua from whence the terrified enemy fled in panic toward Ojinaga on the road to Coahuila, always fleeing from Villa, who caught them, stopped them, and destroyed them in Ojinaga thereby putting an end to the campaign of Chihuahua."

Venustiano Carranza, First Chief of the Revolution
(Courtesy of the John O. Hardman Collection.)

---

[5] Mexico had been warned by the United States about violating the border. Villa was careful not to fire directly north toward the Rio Grande into El Paso. SEH

However, the phlegmatic Porfirian Governor of Coahuila[6] does not allow anyone in the Revolution who has prestige greater than his. He has alienated and continues to alienate from his inner circle all men of worth. Carranza now met the strategic military triumph by Villa in Chihuahua with contempt and political intrigue. But independent of Carranza, the successful actions of the Revolution were overwhelming and the military prestige of General Villa grew.

Very soon Villa's increasingly numerous and now seasoned troops of the North were fighting formal battles that exhibited eloquent examples of daring strategy.

Torreon:

In Torreon by perseverance Villa led 10,000 men with 30 canons through ten long days of terrible fighting, and forced the enemy of about equal strength to evacuate that city. That victory was completed by a battle in the nearby town of San Pedro las Colonias where an effectively superior enemy was defeated and sent fleeing south in disarray toward Zacatecas.

At the key point of Paradon about 5,000 federal troops tried to block the passage of Villa's Division del Norte toward Saltillo. A military disaster consumed that vanguard in a few moments and forced the evacuation of Paradon. Senor Carranza planned to bring his apathetic presence to the capital of Saltillo, the city that the strong arm of Francisco Villa had conquered for him.

The Division del Norte increased greatly in fighting numbers along with the prestige of its *Jefe* and prepared itself for the most decisive triumph in the recorded history of Mexico. But Carranza's jealousy grew with each increase of Villa's prestige because the light of his military success illuminated Carranza's passive smallness. Carranza forged machinations in concert with General Pablo Gonzalez in Monterrey and prohibited Villa from going to Zacatecas where he

---

[6] The term 'Porfirian' refers to the reign of dictator Porfirio Diaz. Carranza was governor of Coahuila during the 30-year reign of Porfirio Diaz. SEH

might reap a new triumph. Villa nevertheless, obeyed his superior duty to his generals, and in spite of Carranza's obstruction moved his Division del Norte to Zacatecas.

Telegram:

"We have convinced General Villa", said all the generals of the Division del Norte in a telegram to General Carranza, "The promises we made to the nation obligate us to continue the mandate of the Division del Norte as if you had not taken the malevolent resolution of depriving our democratic cause of its most prestigious Chief in whom liberal and democratic Mexicans have placed their most cherished hopes; If we listen to you the Mexican people who long for the triumph of our cause, would not only anathematize you for such an insane decision but also for insulting the man who leads us to liberate this country from brutal oppression by our enemies.

We will not abandon our arms in order to subject ourselves to a principle of obedience to a Chief that is destroying the hopes of the nation with your dictatorial attitude, your promotion of disunity with the United States that runs the risk of a misunderstanding in our foreign relations.

We fully understand that you were hoping for an occasion to extinguish the sun that dims your brilliance. But contrary to your desire to have no powerful man in the Revolution who is not an unconditional *carrancista,* are those of the Mexican people to whom the prestige and victorious sword of General Villa are indispensible."

The Battle of Zacatecas is particularly notable because it appears as the first almost classic encounter of the Revolution or even of the history of Mexico. It presents all the phases: preliminary reconnaissance, making contact with the enemy, tightening the circle around the site, distribution of troops, choice of positions and establishment of batteries of artillery as well as the effective use of it in support of other arms, designating a reserve, choosing the main point of attack, managing the regular pre-planned unfolding of the battle, the assault of the strong positions, and the final effort and effective follow through.

The quality of the defensive positions seemed impregnable, and the actual combatants were the following: 12,000 men defended the enemy position while 20,000 men were attacking, besieging it.

The Division del Norte assaulted and took six entrenched and dominant hills and routed the garrison of Zacatecas in nine hours of fighting.

Description:

The city of Zacatecas, capital of the State of the same name, is situated on the Central Plateau of Mexico at an altitude of 2,400 meters (7,200 ft.) in a deep canyon surrounded by tall mountain peaks. The city has an exquisite and refreshing climate in summer.

Because of the topography of the land, the city has lengthened itself from North to South, filling up the central area with two-story buildings to compensate for lack of width. The city appears to wind like a serpent through the canyon and expands by creeping up foothills hills of the peak La Bufa on the East, and up the slopes of Las Bolsas and the foothills of the eminence El Grillo on the West.

In order to enter Zacatecas from the North one must go around a barrier formed by these mountains that are more than 300 to 500 meters (1,000 to 1,500 feet) higher than the City.

Veta Grande, a mine and village of the same name famous in earlier times, is hidden behind these two mountains and alongside this small, sad, semi-abandoned village runs a wagon road that comes from Morelos and heads toward the Capital city of Zacatecas searching for favorable gradients of land by curling around hills and heading South until it enters the Northernmost part of the City.

Another cart road from the East comes from Aguascalientes, passing through the village of Guadalupe, seven kilometers from the Capital, and entering by a moderate slope ascending through the canyon that separates the *Altiplano* peaks from La Bufa. This last is memorable for the assault that General Rocha made in 1871 when the frontier generals defended Zacatecas against the legitimate government of President Juarez.

A third road leads from the Southwest to the Capital (the road from Jerez) winding around foothills and arriving at the Southern most point of the city where the railroad track enters and the railway station is located.

These three roads radiating from Zacatecas, to the North, the East and the South, constitute the roadways that communicate with exterior cities.[7]

The railway substantially parallels the path to Guadalupe, to the South away from the City.

Going from Veta Grande to Zacatecas from North to South there is an immediately sharp elevation that marks the beginning of the City. In the background like a rearguard facing toward us is a strongly fortified red hill of medium height (Loreto), and to the side a flanking guard provided by a high and elongated mountain in the shape of a spine called Cerro El Sierpe.

Close by and framing the City are two Colossi protecting her. On the East side rises an up-thrust called La Bufa with inaccessible sides, fortified with artillery and dominating the valley with an observatory at its peak surmounted by a spotlight. Parallel to La Bufa and facing it is another elongated hill that protects it and is of prime importance because it must be taken before getting close to La Bufa.

On the West, rounded and also dominant, rises a second Colossus, Cerro del Grillo, an important height that is key to the position. It has been carefully fortified with artillery and has abundant infantry.

Finally to the South rises a high hill in the shape of a cone, Cerro de Los Clerigos, where a garrison of troops is hiding.

One of these three roads must be taken to reach the City that is surrounded by strong natural elements, well fortified and garrisoned

---

[7] The road to Morelos in reality divides into two at the exit of Zacatecas, one going in the direction of Fresnillo to the East, and to the Southeast there are also two roads: from Jerez and from Villanueva. FC.

with more than 10,000 soldiers. One must be chosen and the heights previously controlled.

Preliminaries:

The troops of the Division del Norte arrived from Torreon and camped a day's march from Zacatecas, placing them where they could approach the outskirts of the City.

Later, General Ángeles and his staff began an offensive reconnaissance, with an escort of twenty men. In San Vincente a column of 200 soldiers patrolling the outskirts of the City engaged the Ángeles patrol. The battle was on the point of turning against us when, fortunately, we were aided by the arrival of General Trinidad Rodriguez with his troops who repelled the enemy and pursued them as far as their defensive position.

Various reconnaissance made previously showed us that the Southwest the foothills that guard the City were well battered by fire from several emplacements. This suggested they were wisely chosen and would likely be the strongest point of the defense. The North, in contrast, is an undulating area dominated by fire from the various high places.

General Ángeles liked this northern front and selected it as the most appropriate for the main attack because from there our artillery would face enemy artillery and because it could also give strong support to the infantry that would have to assault the high strongholds.

General Headquarters of our artillery and the Ángeles Brigade remained established in Veta Grande.

The selection of main positions for the artillery was made two days in advance.

Our troops in these positions suffered a cannonade passively last night and the night before. The partial combat in the Northeast by the troops of General T. Rodriguez and in the Southeast by those of M. Herrera, show from the number of casualties suffered (especially among the troops of that last general: Herrera was wounded on his arm, and by the damage caused on the artillery: two pieces were knocked off their mounts, gunners were killed and wounded), that the enemy artillery had the distances and references to these positions measured beforehand.

On the 22nd of June the order was given that on the following morning at 10:00 a.m. our artillery would open fire on enemy positions and the forces of the Division del Norte, commanded by General Villa, who arrived just that evening and was fully aware of the situation, would begin the attack.[8]

Our infantry would remain in separate formations and attack in the following order: from the Northeast, taking the position in front of La Bufa and the road that leads to Zacatecas, the brigades Ceniceros, Morelos (General Urbino), Robles (General Benavides), 3rd Battalion (Col. Gonzalez) with part of the Zaragoza (General Madero) made an effective total of about 3,000 men. In the North was the first part of the Madero Brigade linked to part of Ceniceros with 1,500 men; from the Northeast came brigades "Villa" (J. Rodriguez), and Cuauhtemoc (T. Rodriguez and Rosalio Hernandez), with a total of 4,500 men; From the East came Zapadores of General Servin and troops commanded by General Almanza with some 2,500 men. In the South and Southwest were brigades Herrera, Ortega, and Chao with 3,000 men. And in the East, spread out as far as Guadalupe, the troops of Generals Arrieta, Natera, Banuelos, Dominguez, Triana and Carrillo with some 6,000 men. These last troops had been appointed by the village of Guadalupe, to cut the track and close the pass as ordered by General Ángeles. This blocked the train and prevented troops coming from Aguascalientes to either aid the enemy or to cut off his anticipated retreat.

Natera's troops occupied the mesa las Bolsas in an attitude of waiting.

Our artillery was distributed in two parts: the smaller to the South composed of two batteries, with troops of General Herrera ready to support the attack of those or to join the pursuit of the garrison of

---

[8] General Urbina gave the order as *Jefe* pro-tem in the absence of General Villa. FC.

Zacatecas should it retreat prematurely. This was suspected because of a cloud of smoke seen the day before that could have been from fires of the enemy's barbarous custom of burning houses before retreating.

The main artillery group, the one that was chosen to be to be the principle group, did nothing as they faced the battering of enemy artillery (they had been ordered not to fire so as not to be discovered). During the night they moved still closer to the attack point. One part protected itself behind the crest of a hill, the other within the ruins of a half demolished hamlet called Mina La Plata.

This hamlet served as an observation point for General Ángeles in the first phase of the conflict, and as a hiding position for the reserve infantry that would support the principle attack at the indicated hour.

The infantry, in position and ready to attack since the night before, formed a great arc whose extreme ends pointed toward La Bufa on one side and La Sierpe on the other. The hills that faced the hill las Bolsas, another round hill, the hamlet of Eden and other hills on the right together with a few isolated houses constituted the points of the arc of fire that would support them in the principle attack.

The Battle:[9]

June 23, 1914 dawned with clouds and white mist that did little to dim the intense light of the brilliant summer sun. Vaporous mists crawled slowly along the peaks of the hills as if they were reluctant to leave their earthly pillows. The sun managed to escape from time to time to confront the fog, gather it into cottony cumulus, and throw furtive darts of gold to earth. It seemed to peer between the fields and villages where the legion of the brave would collect one more laurel for the Division del Norte and where the bodies of yesterday's heroes lie scattered, decorated with spilled blood, as if they desired to cool the heated blood of those rushing to gain military glory.

---

[9] This part of the record refers to my personal impressions gathered while carrying out the duties as Adjutant of General Felipe Ángeles. FC.

After a tranquil night repairing our forces and gathering new energy and good thoughts about the epic journey that lay ahead, the staff of General Ángeles awoke, breakfasted, and prepared to mount and follow the Chief. A few biscuits slipped furtively into a pocket and some bandages added to the *camarada* bag were the only evidence given of awareness that the battle would be long and dangerous. For the rest, after preparations according to style, such as a morning walk, the General and his officers went to the camp an hour ahead of time.

The troops had spent a rainy night on watch in their advanced positions.

Now the sun had torn off the veil of mist and flooded the camp with light; groups of soldiers could be distinguished as multicolored points scattered here and there.

A fresh breeze from the Northeast had blown away the rain foretold by crashing and rumbling in the neighboring canyons.

The city of Zacatecas spilled out from the depth of the canyon watched over as always by two powerful sentinels, La Bufa and El Grillo. Our covetous glances were directed toward our future meeting place.

The artillery had moved to occupy their new positions.

Preparing to advance we inspected the field, leaving a rearguard to protect the first aid station as well as our horses, and headed on foot toward the destroyed hamlet. It would be our hiding place while the final preparatory orders were communicated.

We had two batteries (Jurado's group) in the main plaza of the destroyed houses where they were out of the sight of the enemy.

Houses on the right and on the left framed other batteries that protected themselves, some with mounds of earth, and others with battlefield trenches that the gunners had constructed during the night.

On the left side another battery of Major Saavedra's Group had advanced, daringly protecting themselves in the same manner as the previous group. Finally, from the height where we had the rearguard on the hill near Veta Grande, two batteries were supporting the first with dominant fire.

Before 10:00 AM the infantry in the front lines entered the conversation of fire with the enemy on El Grillo and La Bufa. Supporting artillery sent a roaring barrage of shrapnel on a cavalry unit they discovered advancing on their position.

We waited the solemn hour with impatience, with the enthusiasm of those who wish to comply with an overriding duty, with the interest of those who wish to discover intense emotions, and with the ambition of those who desire new accolades and new triumphs for their *compadres.*

Protected for now behind two walls, I realized that the enemy could be numerous; until that moment their entire force had not been revealed. The two batteries where we were hiding were going to attract the wrath and the projectiles of the enemy artillery and in a few minutes these walls would be a lot of rubbish. I was happy that our reserve infantry had chosen not to protect itself but was preferring to distribute itself on the front line of fire, and I remembered with curiosity and apprehension the phrases of General Ángeles, "Better they fire at the hamlet because that way they will not be firing at the infantry. We will attract the fire of the enemy canons and…the result will be much happier overall."

The General considered combat like a party to be attended with joy, cleanly dressed for hygiene in case one were wounded, as well as for style. Before leaving he had shaved his beard and carefully combed his mustache.

Moments before 10:00 AM the impatient infantry broke into raging fire with their rifles, and at 10:00 AM exactly, our artillery began to be heard at the party, irregularly at first, but soon in full concert. The red hill of Loreto was our first target. We battered it to protect the assault of the infantry. This valiant advance dislodged the enemy in the trenches on the hillside of that Cerro. The infantry awaited the effects of our canon to enable them to gain distance toward the trenches on top of the hill and soon the first soldiers followed by their flag bearer had planted the tri-color that fluttered happily over the fort of Loreto. This was the first important enemy position to be captured. At the beginning of that assault the brave young General Trinidad Rodriguez lost his life.

During that moment of the fight the hamlet was not destroyed but enemy grenades hit one artillery piece. An alley between two walls served as an observation point. Each of its sides protected us as we observed various phases of the fight. Neither the painfully acute sound of bullets nor grenades exploding near us moved us from the scene.

We saw that to the left our artillery was making good shots in the direction of *Loreto* but they were falling short because our troops were by now halfway up the side of the hill. General Ángeles permitted me to go and give the necessary corrections to Major Roldan whose battery was protecting the valiant Major Saavedra. He improved the shots and made excellent impacts on the trenches atop Loreto. The result was immediately apparent and I left him content.

The taking of Loreto took twenty-five minutes.

I was back at that battery mentioned when General Urbina arrived on horseback. He had observed the combat and asked for General Ángeles. I told him where he could be found and asked him not to go there with his mounted escort so as not to attract enemy fire; several gunners had just been wounded.

At the same time our infantry to the left, supported by batteries on that side, pushed back the group that was in possession of the hill in front of La Bufa forcing them to retreat to La Bufa itself. There they established themselves strongly on the crest they were protecting. From one of the other hills they set up healthy fire and held it for a long while.

Shortly after I returned to the hamlet General Ángeles told me that the batteries that were hidden had been immobilized and that he had sent Capitan E. de Monteros to see if there was a quick remedy.

General Ángeles sent me to look for our horses so we could move to a new area of the fight. Other batteries continued to fire.

When Cerro de Loreto fell to us the focus of the battle turned to Cerro de la Sierpe.

General Ángeles ordered artillery to advance and soon his staff arrived at a gallop at the new theatre of epic battle.

Passing by the battery of Capitan Durón, General Ángeles ordered them to fire at the new zone and a little later in the middle of the road we met General Villa followed by his escort, also coming at a gallop, searching for General Ángeles and asking that artillery dislodge the enemy from *la Sierpe*. General Ángeles assured him that he had already ordered the advance.

We all went in a group toward the dangerous area. Surrounded by a halo of prestige General Villa led the column, imperturbable, showing his strong martial character, conversing amiably with General Ángeles who accompanied him. Following on foot behind our chiefs were both staffs. It did not take long for a hail of bullets to come actively seeking victims among our highly visible group of faithful men following the two brave and notable generals.

The aide and the horse of Major Bazan were wounded, but the two groups continued at the same slow, imperturbable pace of their chiefs.

I had gone to order all functioning batteries to advance and fire at the new enemy position. Capitan Durón questioned my order somewhat because his shots were on target and because he had just received contrary verbal commands from General Ángeles. I explained that my order was more recent and was overriding. I continued on to the hamlet in front of *Cerro Loreto* (the mine of the same name) from which a deep valley separated us.

Generals Villa and Ángeles and those accompanying them had arrived there.

Enemy artillery fire rained down on the houses and vicious bullets whistling by removed all desire to even peek over the edge of the wall that sheltered us.

The General climbed to the roof to better observe the situation. I went with him and after sufficient exposure he invited us to get down and the firing raged on.

Troops on the right were firing with enthusiasm and in one vigorous push climbed half way up the side of the steep slope of La Sierpe forcing the enemy at the top to protect themselves in trenches and strong stone fences.

The steep incline of the climb and the speed of the thrust forward drained our troops and they began to flag. The enemy rallied, came out of their trenches, and was beginning to push our men backward.

A machinegun located in an angle of the houses since the beginning of the fight tried to help our troops with its rapid fire but without having much effect.

The defenders of La Sierpe stood up and fired directly at the bravest of our men who were standing just a few steps from them. Our fighters were desperate and the moment, serious. Those in our group turned their faces toward us pleading for artillery. The general ordered me to run and bring even one canon, I went for it and a few minutes one canon, followed by a second was placed in battery and the weapons uncovered immediately.

Everyone watched the canons anxiously and in suspense awaited the results. I helped to aim the first one with the valiant Captain Durón who took command of his section with me there to observe the canons effectiveness and soon we fired a second shot. Our grenades struck in the middle of the enemy. We didn't have to wait for results. The enemy began to run and our troops advanced boldly. Immediately bravos and applause were heard all around us along with the fanfare of *dianas*[10] accompanied by *viva's,* and shouts and tears of emotion as the flag fluttered over La Sierpe.

From the moment of the first artillery attack this position had taken fifteen minutes to fall.

We continued to fire, following the enemy in retreat.

Wasting no time, the canons were advanced resolutely as far as an uncovered area in front of the house. The gunners redoubled their efforts and battled furiously with canon shots at the hill of El Grillo.

---

[10] *Dianas* are musical riffs played in celebration at bullfights and other public events. SEH.

Both El Grillo and La Bufa answered us with shots that were sometimes long while others were short and only the dust of their explosions reached us. However a grenade hit near one piece and caused casualties. But that grenade did not stop their firing; while bullets whistled the gunners prepared, armed and fired.

As Generals Villa and Ángeles and some officers including myself neared one canon that was firing accurately, we climbed atop a pile of rocks to have a better view. Suddenly a few feet from us came a blast stronger than the noise made by the piece we were observing. It blinded and deafened us and covered us with dirt and smoke. Stunned, we heard cries of horror and groans or rather shrieks of a seriously wounded gunner.

'They have hit us with a grenade,' was my first thought, but as the smoke began to clear I could see a pathetic picture. Surprisingly, thinking back at that moment, it caused me no emotion at all. Near us and behind the canon we found the mutilated remains of a gunner (the arranger of the fuses), with his hands blown off and his face and head destroyed. To one side were standing other wounded men covered in blood and full of fear and pain. When the crews realized the situation they ran in panic in all directions.

Seeing the shock in their faces that were twisted with terror General Ángeles gathered the gunners to their cannons and strengthened them with shouted commands reminding them of their heroic duty.

To complete this emotionally fraught picture, a group of about twenty gunners with panicked faces pale as death, backs bent to stay protected by the wall behind us and out of the line of fire. The General was indignant with them, called them cowards and ordered them to the front where their companions were fighting. They half obeyed, crouching on all fours and sidled sideways like crabs to avoid danger. The general rebuked them and took out his revolver to threaten them.

I seconded him, and at last the men conquered their fear and went to join their brave companions.[11]

Meanwhile the fight continued but the intensity diminished. The artillery continued to batter El Grillo but our troops did not advance any further.

Major Fierro appeared with his leg pierced through, temporarily leaving the scene.

General Villa wanted to continue the advance of our troops up El Grillo and lacking his assistant for the moment, decided to go himself to give the order to the troops. General Ángeles guessed my thoughts and decided that I could go in his place. General Villa accepted and I galloped off toward the front line[12]

Bullets welcomed my way, whistling capriciously and augmenting the discomfort of my horse that was already bothered by the still warm corpses lying in the field about us.

In some small houses at the front I found troops that were firing from protection of mounds of earth. I shook hands with some of the officers (E. M. Santos Coy, Colonel Alborez and others), and it happened that I met General Madero there. I told him that General Villa wanted all troops to advance and asked if this would be a good time for him to move. He answered that his troops were now so few and their supplies so depleted that this was not a good time. He asked General Villa to send reinforcements.

I returned at a gallop, listening to the whistling of bullets, long and wailing, or short like a click. My instinct told me bullets that did not respect my face would not turn traitor and respect my back. One of them hit the ground between the feet of my horse causing him to leap on all four legs and gallop faster.

At last I arrived to communicate Madero's report to Generals Ángeles and Villa.

---

[11] Dear soldiers from the village...said General Ángeles in his notes...obligated to be heroic, when their souls are trembling and their legs are weakened. FA.

[12] We could see him in the distance, with his hat tilted to one side, galloping rhythmically on his sorrel. FA.

There were no reinforcements and the troops were exhausted.

El Grillo was beginning to be cleaned out by the efforts of our artillery.

It was one thirty in the afternoon when the intensity of the firing died down.

La Bufa had been silenced, and troops called a truce.

The first great phase of the battle ended when the positions in front of La Bufa: Cerro de Loreto and La Sierpe were conquered.

Now, in the South fire from the enemy artillery was plummeting down on troops of Herrera, Chao, Ortega, and Servin and fierce fighting could be heard from there that proclaimed the force of the battle.

Second Phase:

From within the house where we were, near a house that had been burned by the enemy, we could see the scenes I have described through a hole blown in the wall by an errant grenade. Baca, the assistant of General Ángeles, brought us a meal that we enjoyed with General Villa and other officers. We ate well accompanied by explosions of canons. After lunch General Ángeles and I walked outside and discovered an unfortunate horse. A grenade had ripped off his right leg. We put an end to his life with our weapons. The shots from our pistols seemed insignificant to our ears deafened by so many canon blasts and by incoming explosions around us.

Taking advantage of the truce, we mounted our horses and headed to the left to see the extent of the progress made on that side.

On the way, seeing that victory was imminent, General Ángeles ordered me to take a written message to Captain Quiroz whose guns were still firing. The message said: "Go and take a position at El Grillo. You will receive orders there".

The position taken by our troops on the left remained strongly occupied and continued to exchange a healthy rain of fire with the well-protected troops on La Bufa.

Their canon continued its fire, now to the South, now toward Loreto.

The hill of El Grillo had been free of enemy troops for about an hour. But now, little by little, we could see that numerous troops were returning to occupy it and to recover their canons. Soon they would erupt in fire once again.

Our troops had taken a breath. The artillery, mainly the battery of Quiroz, now established in the Loreto mine, battled the forces on El Grillo with renewed fury and in no time we could see first a few men retreat on foot, later larger groups retreating and last, a whole human chain rushing from the hill to get into Zacatecas. Our artillery fired at them as they descended.

At 5:50 in the afternoon we saw a huge pillar of smoke rising from the City and General Ángeles said, "They are burning the City." Engineer Valle standing with us said, "from the position of the smoke it seems to be near the market and the way the smoke is dissipating quickly suggests an explosion rather than a fire." His conclusion was later confirmed.

Moments later our troops advanced, scaled and occupied the stronghold of El Grillo, where they planted two victory flags.

Meanwhile, in the South, the combat raged on in the camp of our compatriots. I could see that the enemy there was also retreating toward the City forced out by the thrust of our troops on that side

The mount of Los Clerigos, the object of harsh attack, had probably fallen into our hands.

We advanced a battery on our left wing, which began to fire at short range against La Bufa. From there the enemy began to shoot radially in all directions. Foreseeing that they would soon be firing on our battery, General Ángeles told to us to protect ourselves in a hollow and soon the projectiles from La Bufa sailed over our heads. Similarly, flying *zumbadores* broke apart resounding sinisterly behind our advanced position. The only way to anticipate the shot beforehand was to be attentive to the flash.

The artillery on La Bufa changed the direction of its fire thinking that another enemy even closer was threatening them, so we were able to turn our attention to the left and the road to Guadalupe. There we discovered with joy that numerous mounted enemy troops were galloping toward that village. A little later they returned in groups searching for a way out. The troops that were posted on the road to Guadalupe had cut off the retreat of the enemy and were destroying them. Finally in total disarray they abandoned the road and simply milled around like a herd of sheep.

From our observation point we could seek them out and we called our soldiers to direct their fire toward them, but an officer pointed out to us that we also had soldiers going around on that side who could be wounded. We suspended that plan and merely observed.

General Ángeles sent a message to General Villa, "We have won".

Meanwhile our artillery made accurate shots on La Bufa and they no longer responded. The people there began to move and our infantry started to climb the hill.

The formations in the South increased their attack and the enemy fled on the road toward Zacatecas where the enemy occupants of El Grillo descended to meet them.

Finally the enemy fled from La Bufa toward the road to Guadalupe.

Artillery fire had ceased but we heard healthy fire inside the City.

Our troops were entering Zacatecas amid blood and fire.

I obtained permission from General Ángeles to go forward into the City with the enthusiastic Engineer Valle to look for lodging.

Since I had experienced the emotions and the magnificent panorama of the beautiful battle in the field with my comrades focused on the enemy positions I also wanted witness the last phase of the battle in which the defeated troops fled in complete disorder and the victors also in complete disorder entered the City and conquered the last hurdle.

On the way we picked up some stragglers and with our weapons ready for any event, we entered the City at seven in the evening still lit by the last rays of the sun of a magnificent summer day.

Corralled and defeated, the enemy soldiers were either dead or taken prisoner.

The people of the outermost areas of the town were peeping fearfully from behind doors and windows. But from the center of the City we could hear shouts and shots being fired, *dianas* playing and sounds of total confusion. At least 10,000 victorious men invaded a totally unknown city, a city with hermetically sealed doors and windows.

I smelled dust and human flesh.

Cadavers were lying in blood in the streets; victors were pounding on doors with rifle butts and were shooting at windows leaving shards of glass littering the streets. Telephone and telegraph wires strung across the ground made it difficult to traverse.

Groups of men were disputing and dragging carriages through the streets that they had found or had just taken from garages. The victors looted some stores. The following day they would pay with their lives for their robberies (There were 60 executions for looting.)

In the center of the City that the military multitude had been able to reach we found debris of a great building: the Bank of Zacatecas and *Jefatura de Armas*. Houses in front and on each side had windows broken, balconies broken apart, walls cracked and blackened by a formidable explosion.

Destruction by Federalists, June 1914
(Courtesy of the Historical Archives of Zacatecas)

The barbarians called federalists, the supporters of the assassin Huerta, destroyed everything they could, including the inhabitants, as a final act of revenge.

But the garrison of 12,000 men atoned for this last crime with their annihilation.

The Outcome:

Fleeing disorder and danger from shots being fired in the air, *dianas* playing, flashes from guns being fired from dark alleys where sinister shadows lurked, we took refuge in the house of some prominent people, pale with terror, who opened their doors to us.

They provided us with a frugal meal and when the hubbub died down a bit one of them bravely went out into the street with me so that I could look for lodging.

It was a starlit night but dark, barely allowing us to see cadavers. At each step of our horses shied in fear. Men who had not found shelter were stretched out in doorways and gardens.

In the main plaza, the *Plaza Independencia*, many victorious soldiers were sleeping seated with knees drawn up, alternating with corpses for neighbors that slept an eternal sleep.

Life and Death joined hands in a macabre dream of war on that starlit night.

That night I slept deeply.

The next day I went to the road to Guadalupe to see the result of the result of our artillery. A brook and fields that bordered the road were littered with military caps and jackets, etc. as well as with cadavers. They gave a vivid picture of the extreme struggle.

The macabre psychology of death could be studied in the abundance of dead from their gestures and positions. Some bodies looked natural suggesting a merciful death, but most had expressions of the same grim despair with which they were fleeing. Arms were covering their faces as a sign of terror or pleading mercy. All were demonstrating the horror of their last moments. Some had met death instantly like someone who has been thrown from a horse, with hands stretched out laterally in a violent gesture. Some bodies had their heads hidden in their arms, their bodies crushed to death. I saw one that had a military cap on his head (a useless joke) another showed the stripes of an unknown Capitan on an upraised arm.

The majority died of head wounds.

Among the cadavers we saw bodies of women and children.

Many were officers whose rank could be identified by the quality of their underwear, especially by their socks. Their outer garments had completely disappeared.[13]

A drunken man was celebrating his revenge and his base instincts by shooting a corpse at close range in the bowels....

Next to the fence on a precipice several meters high some riders in their desperate flight had jumped, horses and all crashing to the bottom of the abyss.

We found crossing the area difficult; carriages could barely pass through without running over feet of men or legs of horses. Even the horses showed their horror.

---

[13] And to think that the major part of these dead were caught and impressed by Huerta to be our enemies and by extension friends of ours! And because of the inertia of a flock of sheep had stayed on the side of injustice. FC.

This portrait of horror continued all the way to Guadalupe.

It was said that only eighty to one hundred riders were able to escape from Zacatecas due to excellent horses and luck.

As I returned to the City I found long lines of prisoners occupied with seizing arms and carrying bodies. The wells of mines were filled with cadavers.

On the sides of the road and near the station were piles of cadavers that could not be buried immediately. They were to be burned in a heap.

The City was illuminated by a sinister glow of human bonfires and the odor of burning flesh was strong.

A garrison of 12,000 men was annihilated in nine hours of fighting. Our victory in an epic battle was complete.

The persecution was bloody and the camp looked as though death and desolation had passed through hand in hand; it looked frightening!

The Result:

The terrible defeat inflicted on the army of Huerta in Zacatecas had such resonance that it broke the morale of the enemy. It began the retreat of Huerta's generals to San Luis Potosi to the East and to Guadalajara in the West.

The Division del Norte could march triumphantly into the Capital of the Republic, Mexico City, and now Villa loaned General Ángeles five brigades and sent him to Aguascalientes. However, on the way an unexpected order came from General Villa that we should return to Torreon.

The glorious battle of Zacatecas, a great victory achieved against the orders of *don* Venustiano Carranza had increased his envy of Villa and his fury. Empowered by the army of General Pablo Gonzalez he took an openly hostile attitude toward the Division del North. Instead of congratulations he sent an order to cut of Villa's supply of coal.

General Villa did not want to compromise his line of supply with the border. His locomotives were out of coal and *don* Venustiano would not permit him to resupply.

* * * *

This was the inglorious ending of the Battle of Zacatecas. The Division del Norte was prevented from making a direct march to Mexico City. However, because the Battle of Zacatecas so devastated the power of the federal army, Victoriano Huerta left the country a few weeks later. The parties of the revolution were successful in unseating the usurper but they failed to agree on how to govern the nation. A political battle ensued between the Constitutionalists (Carranza and Obregon) and the Conventionists (Villa, Maytorena and Ángeles) and civil war became inevitable. SEH

APPENDIX
Names of Participants at the Battle of Zacatecas

ALMANZA
GENERAL FELIPE ÁNGELES
MAJOR ÁNGELES
GENERAL BABUELOS
MAJOR BACA
MAJOR BAZAN
MAJOR CALOCA
VENUCIANO CARRANZA
ANGEL CASSO
GENERAL CENICEROS
MAJOR FEDERICO CERVANTES
GENERAL CHAO
GENERAL CONTRERAS
GENERAL DOMINGUEZ
CAPTAIN DURÓN
CAPTAIN ESPINOZA DE LOS MONTEROS
RODOLFO FIERRO
CORONEL GONZALITOS
PABLO GONZALEZ
GENERAL HERRERA
JURADO
LUEVANO

GENERAL RAÚL MADERO
GENERAL NATERA
GENERAL ORTEGA
LIEUTENANT PERDOMO
CAPTAIN QUIROZ
GENERAL JOSE RODRIGUEZ
GENERAL TRINIDAD RODRIGUEZ
GENERAL SAAVEDRA
GENERAL SERVIN
GENERAL TRIANA
LIEUTENANT TRUCIOS
GENERAL URBINA
ENGINEER ENRIQUE VALLE
GENERAL FRANCISCO VILLA

HORSES OF GENERAL ÁNGELES: (each was named for a famous general.)
CURELY
NEY
TURENA

ABOUT THE AUTHOR:
GENERAL FELIPE ÁNGELES

The two accounts of Ángeles and Cervantes are similar because they both describe the same limited number of events. However each account reflects a personal perspective.

General Ángeles was the highest-ranking officer of the Mexican military to join the revolt against the assassin Huerta. He was unquestionably the most educated and most sophisticated officer in the Mexican army at that time. His education included several years at the French military academy of St. Cyr. He was awarded the *National Order of the Legion d' Honneur* by the government of France in 1910.

Ángeles was an irritant to the older established members of the military hierarchy. His incorruptibility was a silent but constant reproach to their culture of mutual corruption.

General Ángeles directed the Military School at Chapultepec and built an officer corps committed to duty, honor, and love of country. His students idolized him; his superiors were annoyed by him and yet, his name was respected by all, nationally and internationally.

His character had been formed by discipline and duty. Politics did not interest to him until he met President Francisco I. Madero. From Madero he captured the vision of a democratically ruled nation. Therefore, when Madero was assassinated it was to Ángeles not merely a crime but the destruction of a dream. That the crime was committed by the army, his own beloved institution, was unbearable and required atonement. He entered the revolt passionately driven to right political and moral wrongs.

Until 1913 Felipe Ángeles had served and excelled solely in classroom settings. He taught and firmly believed that there is an art to warfare. He was versed in the details of planning battles and the use artillery but he had never participated in an actual battle.

Within days of joining the revolution he realized that the leadership in Sonora did not share his passion for ousting General Huerta. Skirmishes fought by them were aimless and poorly planned. More time was spent on dinner parties and photo opportunities than on active resistance. The only general in the revolution that Ángeles respected was the illiterate Francisco Villa whose innate genius was proving successful against all odds.

When General Villa asked the leaders of the revolution for artillery and a general to direct it Ángeles enthusiastically volunteered.

Ángeles joined Villa in April of 1914. The battle of Zacatecas was fought in June of that year. During those few weeks Ángeles built an artillery battalion and established a partnership of mutual respect and trust with Villa.

This diary shows the smooth interaction between the two men and the success of their focused approach to warfare. Ángeles called this battle a masterpiece and a work of art.

ABOUT THE AUTHOR:
MAJOR FEDERICO CERVANTES

Federico Cervantes was a student and great admirer of Felipe Ángeles. President Madero and General Ángeles agreed that Cervantes was the man who would be tasked with the creation of an air force for Mexico. In February of 1913 when President Madero was assassinated Cervantes was studying aeronautics in France preparing for this mission.

When Cervantes learned of the assassination of President Madero he left France and returned to Mexico to join the revolution against the assassin, Victoriano Huerta. Ángeles requested that Cervantes serve as his aide.

In this diary Cervantes makes two points. The first is the difference between men of action, or men of worth as he describes them, and men of the political class, The second point is that the Battle of Zacatecas is unique in the history of Mexico because it is the first classic battle. By classic he means a battle fought using methods of warfare taught in Europe. Until this battle wars were merely a clash of armed mobs. Cervantes believed that science would win battles with planning and strategy. In contrast, Carranza was a believer in non-scientific warfare. He was known to pontificate at his elaborate dinner parties that battles were won by courage and bravery, not by strategy. This view

Immediately put him at odds with both Cervantes and Ángeles.

In his diary Cervantes presents a list of the ten phases of a classic battle. He then provides an example of each of those phases as it was exemplified in the battle of Zacatecas. The result was a victory so complete that the devastated enemy soon collapsed and Victoriano Huerta fled to the United States.

ABOUT THE TRANSLATOR

My interest in aspects of the Mexican Revolution is long standing. It began during years spent investigating the disappearance of my grandfather and his re-appearance on the Mexican border ten years later. That investigation led to *Crossing the Line*, a book published in 2008 with my friend Deloris Huerta Lloyd, and sparked increasing interest in Mexican history. By 2012 I had become entranced with the character of General Felipe Ángeles, a man of outstanding abilities and education chosen by his president to be the director of the Military College of Mexico, the equivalent of our West Point. In order to rescue his nation he willingly and humbly volunteered to become artillery general of the Division del Norte under command of General Francisco 'Pancho' Villa. Pancho Villa was an illiterate peasant gifted with uncommon military instincts. A planned biography of General Ángeles is in process.

Research is often filled with surprises; recently as I looked for information about General Ángeles and his role in the revolution I discovered two original sources...battlefield diaries from the battle of Zacatecas. The diaries are preserved in archives, protected but never translated. That discovery led me to translate them and to visit the city of Zacatecas to see the site of the battle.

Previously my search introduced me to a biography of Felipe Ángeles by Alejando Rosas that I translated and published in the summer of 2013.

From 1960 until 1987 I lived in Mexico City and Guatemala City, where at various times I taught third grade the American School, raised a family, published a small English language newspaper for the American Society, was involved in the Comité de Bellas Artes, the Museo Ixchíl and raised coffee on a *finca* near San José Pinula. Somehow those fragmented experiences combined to create a growing appreciation of all things Hispanic.

Made in the USA
Las Vegas, NV
29 January 2024

85072778R00049